Culture Wars

A STUDIO PRESS BOOK

First published in the UK in 2021 by Studio Press,
an imprint of Bonnier Books UK,
4th Floor, Victoria House, Bloomsbury Square, London WC1B 4DA
Owned by Bonnier Books,
Sveavägen 56, Stockholm, Sweden

www.bonnierbooks.co.uk

All images courtesy of Shutterstock.com
© Studio Press

1 3 5 7 9 10 8 6 4 2

ISBN 978-1-80078-246-4

Written by Susie Rae
Edited by Saaleh Patel
Designed by Nia Williams
Production by Emma Kidd

A CIP catalogue for this book is available from the British Library
Printed and bound in Latvia

Culture Wars

Gen Z vs. Millennial

Susie Rae

STUDIO PRESS

Millennials: Stop generalising us and acting like we're all the same.

Also Millennials: I'm a Gryffindor.

'Only 90s kids will remember...'

Everyone knows what a Walkman is.
Sit down.

Millennials after adding #girlboss
to their Instagram posts.

Millennials on their way to kill another industry.

Gen Z out here acting like they invented the middle part as if Millennials didn't live through the 90s.

When Zoomers make fun
of your side part online.

You know you're cheugy when your jeans are skinnier than your latte.

Gen Z calling Millennials cringe and then uploading their fiftieth TikTok lip-sync video.

Millennials: Everything sucks and nothing matters.

Gen Z: Everything sucks and nothing matters.

Millennials refusing to go out because they paid their rent and want to get their money's worth.

Millennials be like 'adulting is so hard'. You're 35. Calm down.

Millennials rushing to the dancefloor when they hear the words 'coming out of my cage'...

Millennials

Gen Z dunk on Millennials for living in a one-bedroom apartment like they don't still live with their parents.

When Baby Boomers start getting mad at Gen Z instead of Millennials.

Gen Z: *trips over*

Gen Z: *looks at a bowl of fruit*

Gen Z: *does literally anything*

Gen Z: Mood.

Millennials: I just don't get
Gen Z fashion.

Millennials 10 years ago:

Millennials: Gen Z are so cringe with their Fortnite dances.

Also Millennials:

Boomers at 23:

Gen Z at 23:

Millennials: Gen Z are the worst.

Gen Z: Millennials are the worst.

Gen X:

Gen Z: *has the darkest sense
of humour*

Gen Z: *will pick up a tear gas canister
with their bare hands*

Gen Z: *physically terrified of calling
to make a doctor's appointment*

When you spent all your money on avocados and now you can't afford a house.

Gen Z: I don't understand Millennial fashion.

Gen Z:

$$\overline{x}_1 = \frac{1}{n} \sum_{t-1}^{n} x_1^t \qquad HV_1^2 = VAR(S_1) = \frac{1}{n-1} \sum_{t-1}^{n} (x_1^t - \bar{s}_1)^2 \qquad \bar{S}_2 = \frac{1}{n}$$

$$= \frac{1}{n} \sum_{t-1}^{n} x_2^t \qquad HV_2^2 = VAR(S_2) = \frac{1}{n-1} \sum_{t-1}^{n} (x_2^t - \bar{S}_2)^2$$

$$\nu(S_1, S_2) = \frac{1}{n-1} \sum (x_1^t - \bar{s}_1)(x_2^t - \bar{S}_2)$$

$$rr(S_1, S_2) = \frac{cov(S_1, S_2)}{\sqrt{VAR(S_1)} \times VAR(S_2)}$$

$$x(S_1, S_2) = \frac{cov(S_1, S_2)}{VAR(S_2)}$$

$$\bar{S}_2)$$

$$S_1, S_2) \frac{1}{n-1}$$

$$\frac{}{\times HV_2}$$

$$, S_2) \cdot \frac{HV_1}{HV_2}$$

$$= \frac{1}{n-1} \sum_{t-1}^{n} (x_1^t - S_1)^2$$

$$: \frac{1}{n-1} \sum_{t-1}^{n} (x_2^t - \bar{S}_2)^2$$

$$\frac{1}{n-1} \sum_{t-1}^{n} (x^t - \bar{S}_2)$$

$$\frac{cov(S}{VAR(S_2)}$$

$$CH_3 \, COONa + ?$$

$$f(T, \nu) = c($$

$$f = u - Ts \Rightarrow$$

$$Tds = du +$$

40

-50 -40 -30 -20

Millennials trying to work out if they're cheugy.

the entire world is on fire

WW3 is looming

everything is a disaster

Gen Z: This is so sad.
Alexa play Despacito.

When you're sick of Gen Z strutting around like they rent the place.

Gen Z making fun of Millennials for liking wine, like they're old enough to drink alcohol.

Gen Z putting their attachment style in their Twitter bio.

Millennials trying to make a meal
that doesn't include avocado,
oat milk or wine.

What Millennials think Gen Z are:

What Gen Z think Millennials are:

Gen Z: We're the smartest generation.

Also Gen Z: Ate Tide pods for YouTube likes.

Millennials when they get the wrong Hogwarts house on their Buzzfeed quiz.

Millennial: *breathes*

Millennial: I did a thing.

Netflix: Has thousands of hours of new content.

Millennials: Time to re-watch Friends for the 700th time.

Gen Z call Millennials embarrassing and then spend four hours learning a Fortnite dance.

Gen Z out here thinking they invented baggy jeans.

Boomers: Young people are
so bad with money.

Gen Z and Millennials: *gets buyers'
remorse from buying a bag of crisps*

Millennials trying to hang
out with Gen Z.

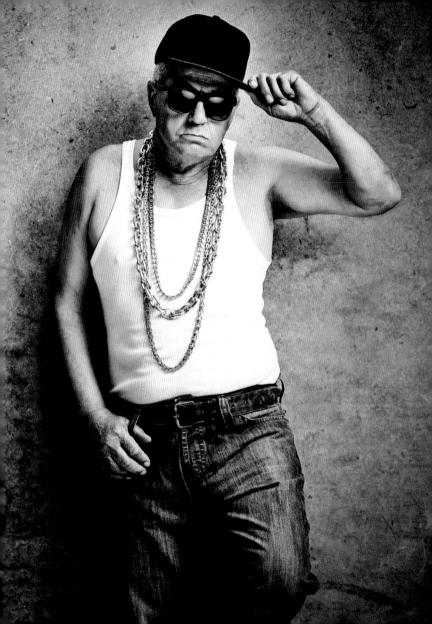

Gen Z will never know the pain of having to stop playing Neopets because your mum wants to use the phone.

Gen Z starter kit:

baggy jeans

bucket hat

vape pen

someone
rolling their
eyes

centre part

Millennial starter kit:

avocado

skinny jeans

side part

Harry Potter-esque robes

'Don't talk to me until I've had my coffee.'

Nobody:

Millennials:

When a Zoomer asks you your birth date and time.

Millennials shouldn't have invented being annoying online if they didn't want Gen Z to perfect it.

Gen Z: It's so embarrassing when Millennials say 'doggo'.

Also Gen Z:

When someone tries to point out that you're in your 30s and are no longer the cool, young generation.

When someone tries to make you
wear low-waisted jeans.

When you spent years training your hair into a side part, only to find out that we're doing middle parts now.

Posting exactly the same
video online three times a day

Gen Z in 10 years' time, realising they're just as embarrassing as Millennials were.

Millennial problems: never being able to read the words 'my wife' in a normal voice.

Trying to get rid of your teenage social media presence before the next generation become old enough to make fun of it.

Gen Z making the same jokes
Millennials made in 2006 and thinking
they invented humour.

When it's 2007 and you've just put 'xXx' before and after your MSN Messenger display name.

Gen Z have never had to wait four hours to download a single song from Limewire, only to find out it's a virus, and it shows.

Gen Z have no idea how
easy they have it.

4, 4, 3, 3, 3,
9, 9, 9, 0, 2,
2, PAUSE, 2,
2, 9, 9, 9, 9

You know you're a Millennial
if you remember when Netflix
looked like this.

Millennials trying to work out what a Snapstreak is.

Making fun of teenage TikTokkers:

Remembering that you used to publicly rank your friends on MySpace:

Realising that there are kids alive whose parents don't remember Finding Nemo coming out.

Gen Z looking for something
new to cancel.

Gen Z making fun of side parts because they never experienced the ultimate hair part.

Making fun of the laughter emoji because you'll never be funny enough to get sent it.

Millennials getting ready
for a night out.

Millennials if someone tries to phone them with no warning.

POV: you're in a
Millennial's bedroom.

Nobody:

Literally nobody:

Not a single person:

Gen Z: